Read All About Numbers

NUMBERS AND COUNTING

John M. Patten, Jr., Ed.D.

The Rourke Corporation, Inc.
Vero Beach, Florida 32964

John M. Patten, Jr. Ed.D.
25 years of professional experience as a writer, elementary and secondary school teacher, elementary school principal and K-12 system wide director of curriculum.
    B.A.—English and social studies; M.ED.—Guidance and education; ED.D.—Education

MATH CONSULTANT:
Mrs. Barbara Westfield, M.S. — Grade Three Teacher

PHOTO CREDITS
Cover and page 18 © N. Hood; pages 4, 6, 13, 21, 22 courtesy of Corel; pages 7, 8, 12, 15, 16, 19 © Zack Thomas; page 12 © J. Patten

Library of Congress Cataloging-in-Publication Data

Patten, J. M., 1944-
    Numbers and Counting / by John M. Patten, Jr.
        p. cm. — (Read all about numbers)
    Includes index.
    Summary: Discusses the development of numbers and systems of counting to answer the question "How many?"
    ISBN 0-86593-438-X
    1. Counting—Juvenile literature. [1. Numerals. 2. Number systems.]
I. Title II. Series: Patten, J. M., 1944- Read all about numbers
QA113.P36 1996
513.2—dc20
                                                96–12628
                                                       CIP
                                                        AC

Printed in the USA

TABLE OF CONTENTS

COUNTING AND "HOW MANY"

Counting is the way most people find "how many." "How many?" can be a very important question.

Think about "how many." A day has 24 hours. Twelve eggs are a dozen. If you have four quarters, you have a dollar.

Let's read about counting and how people learned to find out "how many." It's a good story.

A man counting "how many" dollars he has.

EARLY HUMANS FIND "HOW MANY"

Counting is not something people always knew how to do. Counting was a great discovery and a wonderful tool.

Counting first started thousands of years ago. Early people found ways of counting when they had to know "how many."

Do you think early people wondered "how many" stars are in the night sky?

People first learned how to count on their fingers.

People began counting when they lived in fire-lit caves and wore clothes made from animal skins.

By counting, these early people could keep track of the animals, tools, baskets and other important things they needed for survival. Counting was used long before writing.

FINGERS FOR COUNTING

Do you ever count on your fingers? Of course you do. It is a quick and easy way to find out and remember "how many."

In early times, people probably learned to count by using their fingers (and toes), too. The idea of "how many" started with counting fingers.

In those days, fingers were just counters. They didn't get number names like "one" or "two" or "three" until later.

In early times, people used their toes to count, too.

SCORE

John III

Sue ~~IIII~~ II

COUNTING AND TALLY MARKS

As time went on, more was learned about counting. People began to **tally** (TAL ee) to know "how many." To tally is to make a mark for each thing that is counted.

Tally marks were used long before pencil and paper. Tally marks were lines scratched on dirt or notches cut in wood, or even stone. Pebbles, shells, sticks and other things were used as tally marks, too.

Tally marks helped early people keep simple records of what they had. Maybe the marks gave them ideas about adding and subtracting (taking away). People still use tally marks today.

John and Sue use tally marks to keep score.

SPEAKING AND WRITING

Next, but still thousands of years ago, man's grunts and other mouth sounds started to become simple words. The first spoken language began.

Scientists think that counting words and number names were some of the first words people used. Telling others "how many" was important to them.

These three friends can probably talk and talk.

Ruins of an ancient city in Jordan.

As time went on, cities formed and then came government, science, trade and schools. During these days the writing of numbers began.

In early cities, scribes, or writers, were very important. They made numbers on clay tiles with pointed sticks to keep track of "how many" for all the business of the city. Counting had come a long way from its cave beginnings.

THOSE ROMAN NUMERALS

You have probably seen Roman numerals. They are counting tally marks. Roman numerals were invented in Rome almost 2,500 years ago and were very good for counting "how many."

People do not use Roman numerals for everyday counting any more, but Roman numerals are fun to know about. Here are some numbers that you know and the Roman numerals for them.

1 = I	100 = C
5 = V	500 = D
10 = X	1000 = M
50 = L	

Roman numerals were used for counting until about the time of Columbus' trips to America. They are of no use in modern mathematics because there is no zero.

Today, Roman numerals are seen on clocks and watches, old buildings and, of course, in your arithmetic book.

Roman numerals on the face of a clock.

ARABIC NUMBERS AND ZERO

Arabic numbers, the numbers we use to count, have been around for about 700 years. The number of this page is Arabic; so are your phone number and shoe size.

Arabic numbers are the 0, 1, 2, 3, 4, 5, 6, 7, 8, 9 that you use every day. We borrowed them from the Arabs who got them from India.

The zero in the Arabic number system is why it works. Without the zero, people cannot multiply or divide—important ways to find out "how many."

These are Arabic numbers written in sand.

ABACUS, CALCULATOR, COMPUTER

After fingers, the abacus, invented by the Chinese, is our oldest known counting tool. Like fingers, the abacus is still in use in some places to find out "how many."

Banks have amazing money counting machines. Pour all different coins in the top; and the machine will count them, wrap them and tell you how many dollars you have.

These children are using an abacus for counting.

Using a computer to add Arabic numbers.

Maybe you have used a battery or solar-powered calculator to help find "how many." A calculator is a machine that does **basic arithmetic** (BAY sek uh RITH muh tik)—adding, subtracting, multiplying and dividing—and other calculations.

Personal computers (PC's) are among the world's best counting machines. A PC not only adds 1 + 1. Some PC's can tell you that a **centillion** (sen TIL yen) is a 1 followed by 300 zeros. Ask your teacher if you can write 1 centillion on the board.

MORE NUMBER FACTS

Numbers that tell you "how many" are called **cardinal** (KAR din el NUM berz) numbers. This book is about cardinal numbers.

Our friend, the zero, is called the most important number ever invented because it makes a space with no other number in it. Zero is used in numbers like 102, 209, and 1001.

Numbers go on and on without end. This is called **infinity** (in FIN eh tee). There can be no biggest number, no last number. You can always add one more—always.

For safety, early humans needed to know "how many" wolves roamed near their camp.

GLOSSARY

basic arithmetic (BAY sek uh RITH muh tik) — adding, subtracting, multiplying and dividing

cardinal numbers (KAR din el NUM berz) — numbers that tell you how many

centillion (sen TIL yen) — 1 followed by 300 zeros

infinity (in FIN eh tee) — numbers go on and on without end

tally (TAL ee) — make a mark for each thing that that is counted

People learned to count "how many" thousands of years before this Egyptian pyramid was built.

INDEX